THE SUPERNATURAL

BY

RHIANNON LASSITER

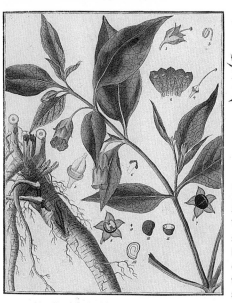

BLACK HATS & BROOMSTICKS

Women believed to have magic power are called witches. According to folklor witches wear black, ride a broomstick, br magic potions in a cauldron, and have a familiar (spirit helper), often in the form of a cat. If any of this were true, witches would be very easy to identify. In the past, many women in England were persecuted for being witches just because they lived alone or used herbs to cure illnesses. The old superstitions inspired many fictional characters in fairy tales and other literature, such as Shakespeare's play, *Macbeth*.

DEADLY NIGHTSHADE

When consumed or smoked, some plants have properties that cause people to have fearful visions or strange sensations. Belladonna (deadly nightshade), a poisonous herb, was often used in magical rites. It can cause the hallucination of flying, which may be why some people believed they were witches and confessed to having flown by magical means.

FOOD FOR THOUGHT

The author Arthur C. Clarke wrote: 'Any sufficiently advanced technology is indistinguishable from magic.' Many of the things we take for granted – radio, computers, and aeroplanes – would have seemed magical to our ancestors. It is human nature to look for explanations for what we do not understand, and 'magic' can be used to explain almost anything! It may be that there are new sciences, not currently known to us, which could explain some of these phenomena. And perhaps the idea of magic is more attractive to us because we have no explanation for it?

THE COURT MAGICIAN

An English scholar, Dr John Dee (1527-1608) was a mathematician and astrologer who studied sorcery and practised as a magician at various European courts. He claimed angels had taught him magic spells and *Enoch*, the language which Adam supposedly spoke in the Garden of Eden. Queen Elizabeth I chose January 14 for her coronation because Dr Dee told her that date was astrologically fortunate. A black crystal, which he said had been given to him by an angel, can still be seen at the British Museum.

WITCHES & WARLOCKS

When events and our sense of things seem beyond understanding, humankind has tended to attribute them to the existence of psychic abilities or supernatural powers. Such beliefs are often found underlying religions, superstitions, and mysteries. All through the twentieth century scientists have sought explanations for a variety of psychic phenomena but there remains much to discover and to understand. To unravel their mysteries and evaluate the evidence we must first explore the history of beliefs in the paranormal.

MAGIC OF THE GODS

The priests and priestesses of ancient religions used magical rites in their ceremonies. Gods such as the Egyptian Isis (above) and the Persian Mithras had mysteries into which only their followers were initiated. Becoming one with the god was the main aspiration. Isis was a goddess of love, death, cunning, and magic. Hieroglyphs and magical inscriptions adorned her temples. Because Isis means wisdom, her initiates were expected to be intelligent and reasoning. Plutarch, an ancient Greek philosopher, described Isis worshippers as seekers of the hidden truths behind the gods.

A DEMONIC PACT

Witches and warlocks were suspected of being in league with the Devil who gave them magical powers in return for their souls. Anyone who claimed they could do magic was therefore believed to be unholy. The English dramatist Christopher Marlowe (1564-93) and the German poet Johann Wolfgang von Goethe (1749-1832) both wrote plays about Georg Faust (1480-1538), a legendary German magician who sold his soul in return for increased knowledge. From within the protection of a ritual circle, Dr Faust is shown here summoning Mephistopheles, an agent of the Devil.

WARDS AGAINST EVIL

Many customs and superstitions are based on magic. Most of them are designed to ward off evil influences but also they often ascribe magic powers to certain items. For example a horseshoe hung over a doorway is thought to prevent witches from entering.

BLACK & WHITE MAGIC

Magic practices traditionally fall into one of two categories. Black magic includes magic rites that make use of blood, death, and the name of the Devil. White magic encompasses powers of healing, visions, and some religious ceremonies. Some people practise magic today but, in most cases, without the rituals and formulae used in past. Not all practitioners of magic think of themselves as either black or white magicians. Some consider the study of magic to be a science which can be used for either good or evil purposes. Others deliberately choose to study only white or only black magic.

FOOD FOR THOUGHT

Witchcraft used to be a convenient excuse for misfortune. If a cow fell sick or a field was blighted, it was easier to blame an old woman who lived alone, rather than to accept that you had been unlucky, or even that you had not looked after it properly. Fear of witchcraft spread quickly, and anyone who did not join in the condemnation of witches, might have been accused of being one. This led to massive witch trials such as those in Salem, Massachusetts in 1692, when more than 150 people from one village were arrested in anti-witchcraft hysteria. In seventeenth-century Europe, even a birthmark could brand you as a witch, and 40,000 people were executed in Britain alone – a fraction of the total in Europe as a whole.

CRYSTAL HEALING

It is a long-held belief that crystals and semi-precious stones have magic healing properties. In Egypt, magicians sometimes advised people to eat the powdered remains of magical amulets to cure illness. This belief is still popular today, with crystal healers claiming they can cure minor illnesses. Some even say that crystals are effective against more dangerous diseases. A crystal is simply placed against the skin of a patient but sometimes it is still powdered and ingested.

DEVIL WORSHIP

Witches and black magicians who made pacts with the Devil held ceremonies to worship him. The Black Mass was a corruption of Christian worship designed to summon the Devil and typically involved acts of deliberate evil designed to please him. The Witches' Sabbat was a midnight ritual in which witches and demons danced around a fire. The tradition is probably connected to older Celtic festivals held on May Eve and Hallowe'en. Although the Witches' Sabbat is still held today, it is not necessarily with the intent to summon the Devil. It can also be held as a celebration of birth and new life.

SOLOMON THE MAGICIAN

In the tenth century, King Solomon of Israel was said to be a great magician. The *Key of Solomon*, one of the oldest known books of spells, tells how he *'discovered the secret of how to shut a million satanic spirits in a bottle of black glass, together with seventy-two of their kings'*. The book was used by black magicians because it also told how to make a pact with the Devil, summon spirits, gain fortunes, and extend life. Solomon's Seal (two interlocked triangles) is often used in magic rites.

VOODOO

Voodoo is a religious cult practised in parts of Africa, South America and the Caribbean. It evolved as a combination of Catholicism and West African tradition on seventeenth-century slave plantations. Voodoo followers believe that while in a trance a person can be beneficially possessed by their ancestors or gods. However, it also has a dark side when used in black magic. Voodoo sorcerers claim they can create zombies – people raised from the dead who are subject to the will of the sorcerer and obey his commands. Voodoo dolls are made by sorcerers using hair or nail clippings of a living individual. Sticking pins into the doll is believed to harm the person it represents.

MYSTICISM & MIRACLES

The psychic powers sometimes attributed to prophets and mystics may be believed in religious contexts but their existence has not been proven scientifically. Every major religion has accounts of miracles performed by priests and saints who possessed unusual and powerful abilities. Religious believers claim their god or gods bestow such powers on their followers in times of crisis. The evidence for the existence of miracles is difficult to trust because 'miraculous' events can be faked. However, the evidence is just as difficult to disprove because we understand so little about psychic phenomena.

THE TURIN SHROUD

First displayed in 1353 the Turin Shroud, which has the image of a crucified man imprinted on it, was said to be the burial sheet of Jesus Christ. In 1989, carbon-dating techniques were used to determine its age. Now generally accepted, the results dated the shroud between 1260 and 1390 – centuries later than Christ's crucifixion. However, there have been allegations that anti-clerical scientists faked the carbon-dating tests and the shroud is still venerated as a holy relic.

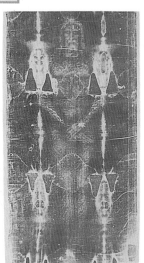

STIGMATA

A well-documented religious phenomenon, stigmata are the five wounds left on Christ after he was nailed to the cross. Since the crucifixion similar wounds have appeared spontaneously on certain people, such as Antonio Ruffini (right). They are generally fervent Christians but have nothing else in common. Stigmata do not seem to be caused by disease or self-inflicted injury. Some people's wounds last for years, others heal quickly. Today, stigmata remain a scientific mystery and are considered by the Roman Catholic Church to be a miracle.

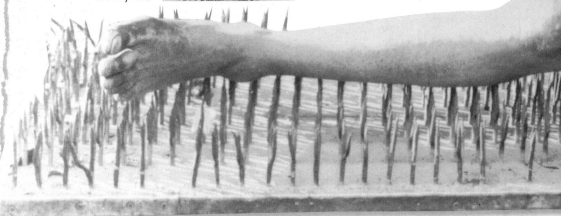

HEALING POWERS

Certain religious statues and paintings are believed to have miraculous powers, capable of healing people of minor and even terminal illness. Every year, thousands of people make pilgrimages to religious sites and for many of them it is their last hope of becoming well. These 'cures' often have an immediate beneficial effect but it has yet to be proved that they make long-term improvements to health. One such statue said to possess the power to heal is the Madonna at Lourdes in France (left).

THE RESURRECTION OF CHRIST

Common to many religions, resurrection is one of the most impressive of alleged miracles. Sceptics who don't believe in divine miracles, or followers of different religious beliefs, sometimes claim that the prophets and demi-gods of ancient religions were people with powerful psychic powers.

FAKIRS

Indian fakirs enter a trance-like state in order to perform astounding feats of endurance. In 1835, the Maharaja of Lahore asked a fakir named Haridas to demonstrate his abilities. Haridas was buried underground in a padlocked coffin with barley sown in the earth above it. Forty days later Haridas was exhumed alive and well. He was never found to have cheated. Fakirs still give displays of their powers, which include lying unhurt on a bed of nails, walking on hot coals and levitation. Although these psychic phenomena have been well documented, scientists are still trying to work out how some of them are done.

MAGIC ENERGIES, PSYCHIC POWERS

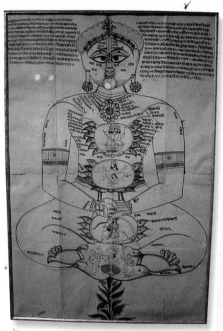

Different belief systems have evolved around occult powers. Some beliefs involve worship and include psychic phenomena as aspects of religious activity. Some people believe paranormal powers are part of normal life and try to live according to complex rituals. Others fear any manifestation of the supernatural and try to ignore any evidence of or reference to it. Our fascination with the paranormal ensures that we will continue to investigate and attempt to understand supernatural abilities and events that do not conform to our existing ideas about the world.

CHAKRA POINTS

Chakra is the Hindu word to describe the main centres of spiritual power in the human body, points along the spine where energy is believed to be transformed into a usable form. Raw energy is said to be drawn from the Earth and fed into the chakra points. There are seven principle chakras in the body and detailed maps of the chakra and their connecting meridians and pathways have been used in Eastern mysticism and medicine for thousands of years.

LEGENDARY TREASURES

Similar to the balance of the elements (earth, fire, air and water) is the traditional pagan belief in four legendary items of great power. In mythology, these treasures are usually a sword, a spear, a cup, and a stone. Each has different powers and stories attached to it. Pagan legends tell of the Cauldron of Dagda, a cup of plenty said to provide a never-ending supply of food. The four objects are also symbols in the Tarot, a deck of cards used in fortune-telling. Magical items feature throughout history. During World War II Hitler collected such objects, believing they would make him invincible.

RITUAL PAINTINGS

The life of the Navaho Indians, a native American tribe who live by the border of Arizona and New Mexico, involves close attention to ritual and magical rites. The Navaho live in harmony with the environment and carry out their daily activities with customs and chants intended to bring good fortune and to ward off evil. One of their most impressive rituals is the curing ceremony, presided over by a medicine man (sorcerer who tends the spiritual well-being of a tribe). It involves drawing elaborate paintings in sand, which they believe helps to cure illness. Rather than magic, perhaps such rituals help to focus the mind. Believing they'll work may be enough to make them work.

CHI ENERGY

The Chinese discipline of *chi* is used in acupuncture healing and in the martial art, *t'ai chi ch'uan*. *Chi* is the energy that exists in all living things. This belief also exists in other cultures and religions. The yin-yang in Taoism symbolizes the two opposite and complementary forces of cosmic energy. Yin is feminine and negatively charged; yang is male and positively charged. Each contains part of the other, as seen in the yin-yang symbol at the centre of this picture of three *t'ai chi* sages. It is possible that a master of *chi* can imbue an object with more *chi*. Uncharacteristically, the Sony Corporation funded a seven-year project into psychic phenomena. These tests included a *chi* practitioner attempting to project *chi* energy into one of two glasses of water. A second *chi* practioner then attempted to identify the glass with more *chi* energy. These tests are said to have had a seventy per cent success rate, but the test conditions and controls have not been verified.

FOOD FOR THOUGHT

Well-established magical systems, such as chi, can be as clearly thought out and consistent as conventional scientific knowledge. In China, for example, acupuncture, a treatment based on the chi system, has been accepted as scientifically valid for hundreds of years. It took a long time for Western doctors to take it seriously as a medical treatment. Other healing systems could offer the same.

BLOOD MAGIC

One belief common to different kinds of practising magicians concerns the power of blood. Black magic ceremonies, voodoo, and African shamanism all include rites that involve sacrificing animals, usually a black cockerel or a goat although other animals may be used.

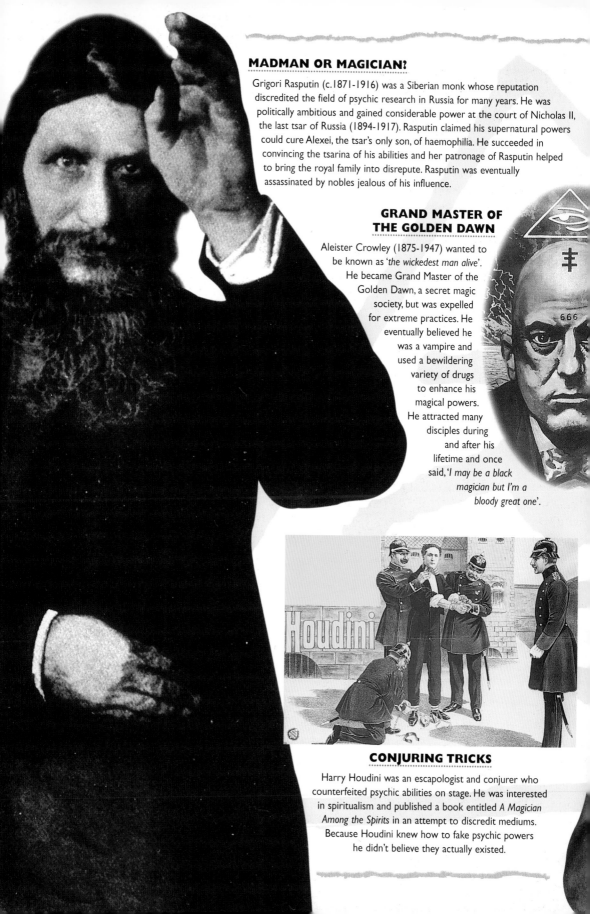

MADMAN OR MAGICIAN?

Grigori Rasputin (c.1871-1916) was a Siberian monk whose reputation discredited the field of psychic research in Russia for many years. He was politically ambitious and gained considerable power at the court of Nicholas II, the last tsar of Russia (1894-1917). Rasputin claimed his supernatural powers could cure Alexei, the tsar's only son, of haemophilia. He succeeded in convincing the tsarina of his abilities and her patronage of Rasputin helped to bring the royal family into disrepute. Rasputin was eventually assassinated by nobles jealous of his influence.

GRAND MASTER OF THE GOLDEN DAWN

Aleister Crowley (1875-1947) wanted to be known as 'the wickedest man alive'. He became Grand Master of the Golden Dawn, a secret magic society, but was expelled for extreme practices. He eventually believed he was a vampire and used a bewildering variety of drugs to enhance his magical powers. He attracted many disciples during and after his lifetime and once said, 'I may be a black magician but I'm a bloody great one'.

CONJURING TRICKS

Harry Houdini was an escapologist and conjurer who counterfeited psychic abilities on stage. He was interested in spiritualism and published a book entitled A Magician Among the Spirits in an attempt to discredit mediums. Because Houdini knew how to fake psychic powers he didn't believe they actually existed.

CONJURERS OR MAGICIANS?

Paranormal phenomena and psychic powers are often faked by conjurers who develop techniques to entertain or deceive their credulous audiences. Some stage magicians freely admit that their feats, such as mind-reading and levitation, are tricks; while others claim their abilities are genuine. Magicians such as Aleister Crowley and Grigori Rasputin managed to convince themselves and other people that their psychic talents were real. But their authenticity is doubted because of the money and sense of power that such magicians gain from their activities.

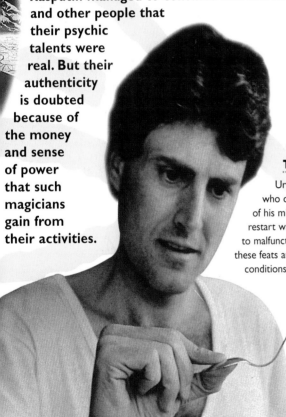

PROFESSIONAL SCEPTICS

A sceptic always doubts and questions accepted beliefs, mistrusts new theories and ideas until scientifically proven and even then tends to think nothing is certain. *Skeptic* Magazine attempts to refute beliefs which in its opinion are '*180 degrees out of phase with reason*'.

THE POWER OF THE MIND

Uri Geller is a stage magician who claims to use the power of his mind to bend metal objects, restart watches, and force computers to malfunction. He has performed these feats and others under strict test conditions but has also been exposed as a fake by people who claim to have seen him falsifying his demonstrations. Since Uri Geller was originally an amateur conjurer, people tend to doubt his psychic abilities.

The phenomenon of metal-bending is not unique to Geller. It has been studied in others who claim to possess a similar power, as well as replicated by metallurgists (experts in metals and their properties).

FOOD FOR THOUGHT

It is impossible to prove that a conjurer does not have magical powers. It may be possible to reproduce the same results by non-magical means but that is not the same. Not many people really believe stage magicians have genuine magical powers, but it is more fun to suspend one's disbelief and enjoy the show. The ingenuity with which some conjuring tricks are devised – levitating, or making a railway carriage disappear – might even be more impressive than if magic were actually being used.

SPIRITS & SPIRITUALISM

People who claim to possess psychic abilities often believe in the existence of spirits – non physical beings who are thought to be gods or the souls of the dead. Some claim they can contact spirits using psychic powers. Spirits can be benevolent, guiding or teaching the humans they care about. But some malicious spirits are believed to return to the physical world to deliberately cause harm. Some spirits are tricksters; amused by the antics of mortals, they play jokes on people who attempt to contact them. Even among spiritualists and practitioners of magic who believe in the existence of spirits, there is no consistent theory about what they are or what methods should be used to communicate with them.

SPIRIT GUIDES

Shamans, like other kinds of magicians, use spirit guides as aids and symbols in their magic. Brazilian shamans believe people have spirits shaped like different animals, the most powerful of which is the jaguar. Native American shamanism involves attuning magic to the path of a different animal. A wolf shaman is expected to be tireless and fierce, while a coyote shaman is a devious trickster. Spirit guides are not necessarily animals. In shamanic magic, strong images and physical symbols are important. The greater the belief in a symbol, the greater its power.

 FOOD FOR THOUGHT

Belief in the survival of the soul or spirit after death has been widespread throughout human history. It seems unbearable to think that we and the people we love will just stop existing when our body dies. And if we do have a spirit that exists independently of our body, why should other things not have one as well?

REINCARNATION

Many people believe that after death our soul is reincarnated (reborn) in another body. Buddhists believe that good or evil deeds in one life will be rewarded or punished in the next. Hindus believe a human who leads an evil life may be reincarnated as an animal. Those who lead worthy lives attain ever-higher levels of enlightenment in each life until they pass on to the next stage of existence. Regression hypnotists have put people into a trance-like state in which they recall events apparently from their previous lives. Some people have even spoken in languages they do not know in their present life. However, it is difficult to prove or disprove the existence of reincarnation.

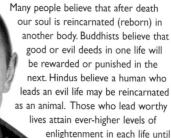

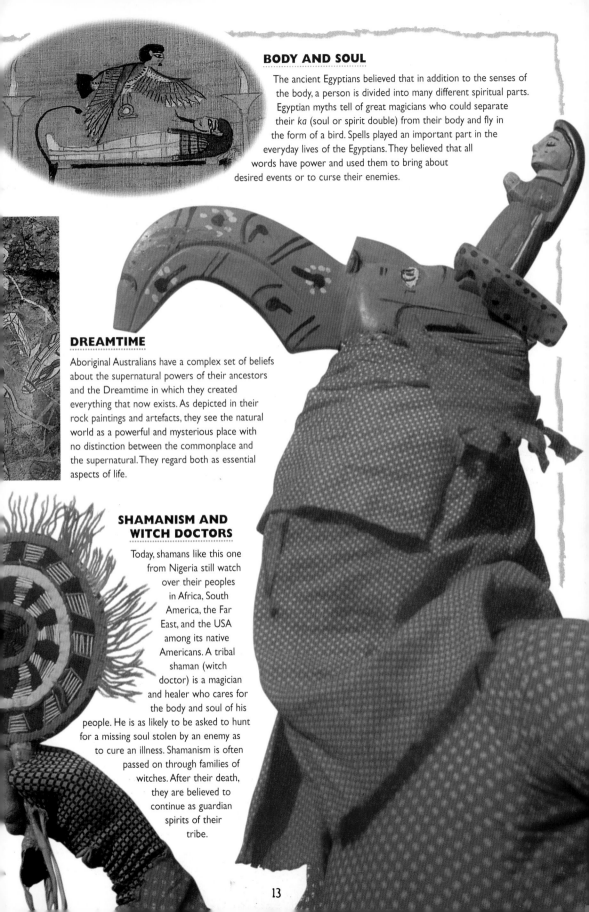

BODY AND SOUL

The ancient Egyptians believed that in addition to the senses of the body, a person is divided into many different spiritual parts. Egyptian myths tell of great magicians who could separate their *ka* (soul or spirit double) from their body and fly in the form of a bird. Spells played an important part in the everyday lives of the Egyptians. They believed that all words have power and used them to bring about desired events or to curse their enemies.

DREAMTIME

Aboriginal Australians have a complex set of beliefs about the supernatural powers of their ancestors and the Dreamtime in which they created everything that now exists. As depicted in their rock paintings and artefacts, they see the natural world as a powerful and mysterious place with no distinction between the commonplace and the supernatural. They regard both as essential aspects of life.

SHAMANISM AND WITCH DOCTORS

Today, shamans like this one from Nigeria still watch over their peoples in Africa, South America, the Far East, and the USA among its native Americans. A tribal shaman (witch doctor) is a magician and healer who cares for the body and soul of his people. He is as likely to be asked to hunt for a missing soul stolen by an enemy as to cure an illness. Shamanism is often passed on through families of witches. After their death, they are believed to continue as guardian spirits of their tribe.

ECTOPLASM

This medium is emitting ectoplasm. Ectoplasm is allegedly a substance called up out of the medium's body to give a spirit physical reality. Silvery-white in colour, it resembles thin fabric and forms the body and clothes of a spirit while it is communicating. Touching a spirit formed of ectoplasm is said to cause the medium to become ill. Although it hasn't been proved that all mediums fake the ectoplasm, it is possible to swallow a skein of cotton and gradually regurgitate it.

REST IN PEACE?

The words Rest in Peace carved on tombstones imply that the dead might not necessarily rest or be at peace. Over the centuries, many stories have evolved about ghosts who do not rest. They haunt people or places for revenge or because they have left something undone in their lives. Some people have reported that they live comfortably with supernatural neighbours. Others say ghosts are dangerous and can smash objects, make eerie noises, and create a perceptible aura of menace in a house.

CLAIRVOYANTS & MEDIUMS

Clairvoyancy is one of the earliest documented psychic phenomena and one of the most lucrative for hoaxers. Clairvoyants and mediums claim that, through them, we can contact the spirit of a dead person. Some mediums only claim to be able to speak with these spirits, others claim they can give them a physical form. Mediums have often been exposed as hoaxers or have admitted to defrauding their clients. A grieving person's fervent wish to contact a dead person they love makes them susceptible to such hoaxes. Although many mediums have undoubtedly claimed abilities they do not possess, clairvoyancy has yet to be fully investigated.

CONTACTING THE DEAD

To contact the spirits, mediums hold a seance. A group of people who wish to speak with a dead person, or perhaps ask about the afterlife, form a circle around a table and hold hands while the medium attempts to summon the presence of a spirit. Mediums have been known to fake the responses of spirits by using devices that strike the underside of the table to produce ghostly knocks in reply to questions. However, some mediums have produced inexplicable effects under test conditions designed by scientists attempting to expose them as frauds.

THE CASE OF KATIE KING

One famous medium was investigated by the Victorian scientist William Crookes. Florence Cook claimed she could manifest the spirit of Katie King (right) who appeared at seances and talked to guests. Florence was suspected of dressing up as the spirit herself or of having an accomplice do so. Crookes asserted that his investigation had convinced him of the spirit's existence. Crookes didn't publish his finding in any scientific journals but he never retracted his claims. Later, it was alleged that he had helped in the medium's fraud in order to have an affair with her.

QUESTIONING THE SPIRITS

It may seem strange today, but in ancient times it was common to ask spirits for advice. Oracles were visionaries who went into a trance to ask questions on behalf of seekers. One of the most famous was Pythia, the Oracle at Delphi in Greece. She used volcanic fumes and drugs to assist her visions. Although ancient and modern mediums have posed many questions to the spirits and entered into long conversations with some of them, no real answers have ever been obtained about life after death or to prove the existence of spirits.

FOOD FOR THOUGHT

If there is life after death, then it would seem reasonable for dead spirits to want to contact the living. Ghosts might be trying to draw attention to the identity of their killer, or to where they buried the family silver. Spirits contacted by mediums might want their relatives to know they are happy and at peace. Some mediums are fakes who take advantage of people who are vulnerable after the death of someone they loved. In their own defence, mediums might say they are only trying to provide comfort for the bereaved. And just because some are fakes it doesn't prove they all are. Some could be genuine.

NORTH AMERICA

BERMUDA

FLORIDA

MIAMI

SAN JUAN
PUERTO RICO

THE BERMUDA TRIANGLE

In 1945, five Avenger bomber planes took off from Fort Lauderdale in America and disappeared without trace near the Bermudas, a small group of islands in the Atlantic Ocean. The boat sent to search for them also vanished. Since then, hundreds of other ships and planes have disappeared in the same triangle of sea. Explanations have included alien abduction, sea monsters and unusual magnetic forces. A magnetic storm could cause intruments to fail, and lost pilots could run out of fuel.

FOOD FOR THOUGHT

The law of probability suggests that out of a huge number of predictions, some of them are bound to come true. Those that don't are quickly forgotten. The same law can be applied to the Bermuda Triangle. In any area of 250,000 square miles, disappearances are not uncommon, and the Bermuda Triangle is an area of extreme weather conditions. Probability could also be a factor in the curse of Tutankhamun – opening a tomb sealed for over 3,000 years could release unknown airborne bacteria. However, people have an appetite for myth and, today, the Internet spreads and embellishes modern myths far more quickly than has ever before been possible. If they are appealing and plausible enough they will spread, whether or not there is any real evidence to support them.

MYSTERY, MYTH & PROPHECY

It is human nature to endeavour to understand the nature of what happens around us. Until we understand unexplained events we cannot make informed choices about how to react to them. Myths usually start after something incredible has happened for which there seems no rational explanation. As science advances, more is understood about the world and how it works. Nevertheless, many mysteries endure. Strange events occur every day and, because it takes time to make sense of them, myths can sometimes grow to epic proportions. Mysteries, like our belief in psychic phenomena, are complex to unravel since they involve the nature of belief itself.

THE CURSE OF TUTANKHAMUN

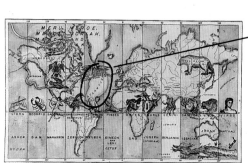

In 1922, the tomb of the Pharaoh Tutankhamun (1336-1327 BC) was discovered by Howard Carter, an archaeologist working for Lord Carnarvon. It is rumoured that Carter destroyed an inscription in the tomb which read: *Death will slay with his wings whoever disturbs the Pharaoh's peace.* A legacy of death did seem to follow the excavation. Lord Carnarvon died in 1923, aged 57. Then an archaeologist, an American financier, and a British industrialist all died after visiting the tomb. During the next seven years 22 more people connected with the discovery also died, many in unusual circumstances. However, Carter himself lived another 17 years and died aged 65.

LOST BENEATH THE WAVES

The lost continent of Atlantis was said to have been the centre of a highly advanced civilization. According to ancient legends, Atlantean scientists under-stood the human mind and were great magicians. Atlantis was said to have been destroyed by a simultaneous volcanic eruption, earthquake, and tidal wave, but some Atlanteans escaped and preserved their magical arts. No convincing geological or archaeological evidence has ever been found.

TITANIC DISASTER

Extraordinarily, some disasters are foretold. Predictions can be recorded before an event, which may seem to prove an ability to foretell the future.

Before major disasters, such as the sinking of the *Titanic*, the calamity is often predicted, sometimes with detailed accounts of what will occur. One theory is that disasters involve so many deaths they create an energy which can be felt by sensitive psychics. This cannot be proven, although many people who do not consider themselves psychic also experience premonitions of danger.

NOSTRADAMUS AND PROPHECIES

Nostradamus was a French doctor known for his treatment of plague in the sixteenth century. In 1555, he published a book of obscure prophecies in the form of quatrains (poems in four lines). His followers believe he predicted various important events of later centuries, but his prophecies are so vague it is difficult to match them to specific incidents. This prophecy was interpreted as foretelling the 1945 bombing of Hiroshima and Nagasaki in Japan: *Near the harbour and in two cities will be two scourges, the like of which have never been seen. Hunger, plague within, people thrown out by the sword will cry for help from the great immortal God.*

BOARD GAMES

Originally called the planchette, Ouija dates from the 1850s and was a triangular board supported by two wheels and a pencil. The pressure of hands placed on the surface moved the board and the pencil wrote messages (apparently from the spirits) on a piece of paper beneath it. In 1868, American toy companies copied and refined the idea to include the letters of the alphabet and the words 'yes' and 'no'. The planchette then only had to move from letter to letter to spell out its message. A Ouija board is a popular way of contacting spirits during a seance, although the messages can easily be faked by players controlling the planchette.

RECEPTIVE MINDS

Meditation is a technique of clearing the mind. Many psychic practitioners use it to prepare their mind to be receptive to telepathic thoughts, or messages from the spirit world. Meditation is also used in prayer, in healing, and as a relaxation technique. Prolonged meditation induces a trance-like state in which all the capabilities of the mind are concentrated on a single thought. Yoga is an Asian meditative technique that has become increasingly popular in the West.

MUSIC FROM THE GRAVE

Some mediums specialize in contacting the spirits of celebrities. Rosemary Brown, a London housewife, claims she has been contacted by the spirits of many eminent composers such as Beethoven who dictated musical scores to her. Experts have said her work is more than just imitation but Rosemary's lack of musical training means she has only been able to retrieve fragments. Another medium, Stella Horrocks, produces whole novels which she claims have been dictated to her by dead authors such as Jane Austen. She goes into a trance to write and the handwriting for each novelist is different.

EXORCISM

Some branches of the Christian Church still perform exorcisms. These rituals are intended not to summon spirits but to dispel them. In the Bible, exorcisms are performed to cast out demons who have possessed a person's body. Nowadays, exorcism is used to dispel ghosts or spirits. An exorcist commands the possessing spirit to depart using the name of God to enforce his injunction. Exorcism, like a powerful spell, requires three items for the ritual – a bible, a bell, and a candle.

CHANNELLING THE SUPERNATURAL

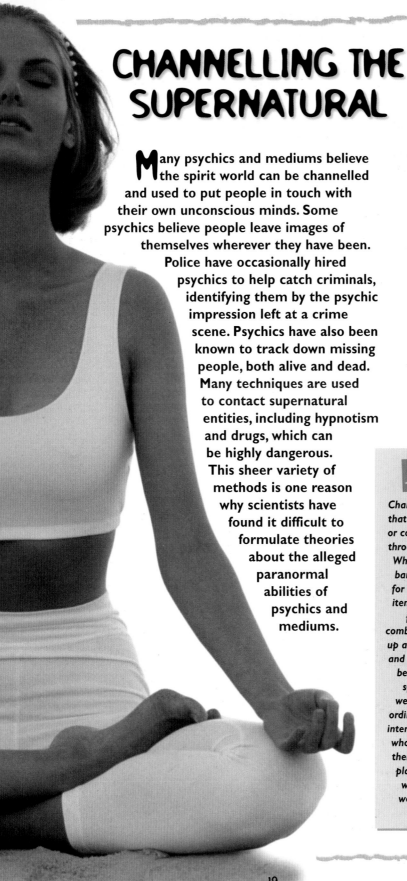

Many psychics and mediums believe the spirit world can be channelled and used to put people in touch with their own unconscious minds. Some psychics believe people leave images of themselves wherever they have been. Police have occasionally hired psychics to help catch criminals, identifying them by the psychic impression left at a crime scene. Psychics have also been known to track down missing people, both alive and dead. Many techniques are used to contact supernatural entities, including hypnotism and drugs, which can be highly dangerous. This sheer variety of methods is one reason why scientists have found it difficult to formulate theories about the alleged paranormal abilities of psychics and mediums.

AUTOMATIC WRITING

Writing without conscious control could be thought of as receiving messages from the spirit world. The subject enters a trance while holding a writing implement and watching the reflection of a candle in a mirror. The writing produced is usually disjointed and incomprehensible but is sometimes treated as if full of meaning. This is not generally regarded as a very credible spiritualist technique because the trance state can easily be faked.

 FOOD FOR THOUGHT

Channelling methods assume that spirits can be controlled or contacted by living people through the power of rituals. Whether they are trying to banish a spirit or asking it for help, people use special items, words, music, mental preparation, or some combination of these, to open up a link between themselves and the spirit. The ritual may be intended to affect the spirit, strengthening or weakening its hold on the ordinary world. Or it may be intended to affect the person who is conducting it, raising their own spirit to a 'higher plane'. It's easier to judge whether something has worked on yourself than on another spirit.

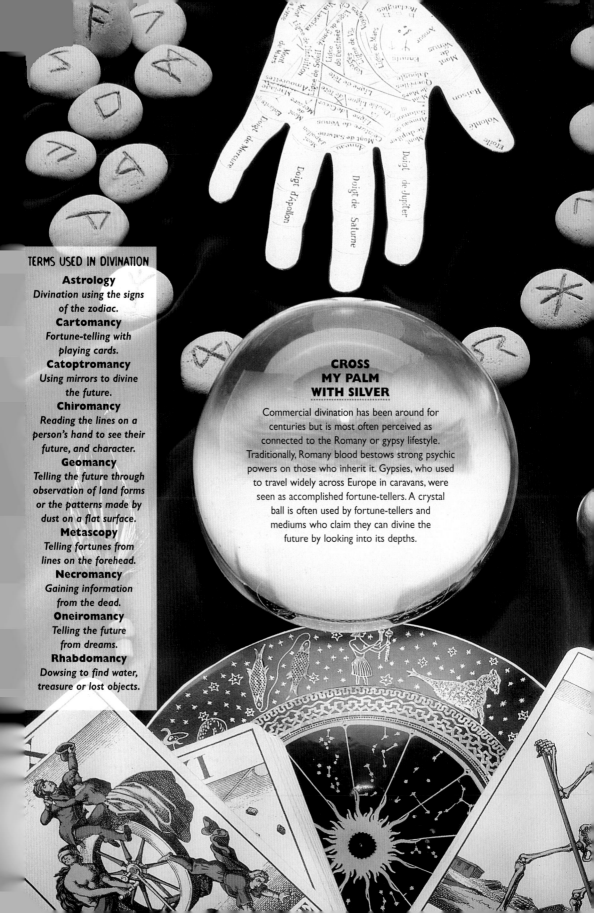

CROSS
MY PALM
WITH SILVER

Commercial divination has been around for
centuries but is most often perceived as
connected to the Romany or gypsy lifestyle.
Traditionally, Romany blood bestows strong psychic
powers on those who inherit it. Gypsies, who used
to travel widely across Europe in caravans, were
seen as accomplished fortune-tellers. A crystal
ball is often used by fortune-tellers and
mediums who claim they can divine the
future by looking into its depths.

DIVINATION

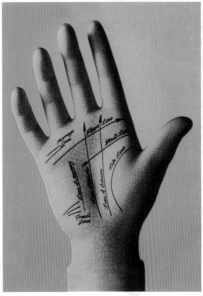

Divination means to foretell the future or, by magical, mystical, or supernatural means, to reveal what is hidden. Many of the divining methods that have been used for centuries are still in use today. Divination often involves a predefined set of symbols which can represent emotions, events, and personal qualities. By selecting these symbols seemingly at random and observing which ones occur in a particular pattern, fortune-tellers make predictions about the future. Other forms of divination involve seeing visions of the future or making observations based on the physical qualities of an individual.

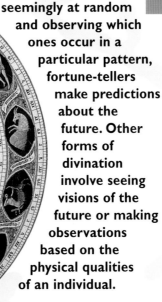

PALM READING

Palmistry, or chiromancy, is a form of divination which involves interpreting the lines on the palm of a hand. Unlike Tarot, Rune-casting, and I Ching, chiromantic predictions are based on an observed quality of the individual. Palmists associate each line on the hand with a different aspect of life. These definitions have developed gradually but are generally held to include: the Life Line, the Health Line, the Line of Fortune and the Line of Fate. Breaks and bends in the various lines signify important events in a person's life.

THE ZODIAC

The Ram, the Bull, the Heavenly Twins.
Next to the Crab, the Lion shines, the Virgin and the Scales.
The Scorpion, Archer and He-Goat,
The Man who carries the Watering Pot and the
Fish with the glittering tails.

This verse, *The Hunt of the Heavenly Host*, helps us to remember the twelve astrological symbols which make up the Zodiac, a system used in several divining techniques. The position of the planets, sun, moon, and signs of the zodiac at the time of a person's birth is believed to define their nature. The signs are divided into four groups associated with the elements, earth, fire, air and water. For example, Leo, a fire sign is associated with adventure and ambition.

 FOOD FOR THOUGHT

Divination or guesswork? Accomplished fortune-tellers can make educated guesses about the future of a client simply by assessing their appearance and personality. Predicting romance for a pretty girl or good fortune for someone who looks prosperous is almost certain to be accurate.

CASTING THE ORACLE

Divination often involves throwing down small objects and reading the pattern they make. Ancient practitioners described this method of divination as casting the oracle. Originally, these methods were used for practical purposes rather than as entertainment and the objects used were simple things that were easily found or made. Over the years, rituals developed around the various forms of divination and the sets of cards, stones, and sticks used became increasingly elaborate and ornamental.

FORTUNE-TELLING WITH TEA LEAVES

Reading fortunes in the tea leaves is not much in favour now that tea usually comes packaged in teabags. Reading the tea leaves is a simple form of divination. Once the tea in a cup has been drunk, the cup is turned anti-clockwise three times. The patterns the leaves form are read to predict coming events. Romany gypsies have a whole symbolic language with which to interpret the images. A padlock, for example, indicates a door to success is about to open.

RUNE STONES

Casting rune stones is an ancient Scandinavian form of divination. The word *runa* means mystery in Anglo-Saxon. Rune Masters were tribal magicians who used the power of their hidden language to affect the weather, the harvest, healing, war, and love.

The traditional Germanic set of runes uses an alphabet of three sets of eight runes beginning with the futhark. Later alphabets contain a blank rune to represent the unknowable. As with cards used in divination, the runes are drawn unseen and laid down in a pattern which allows their symbolic meanings to be applied to a particular question.

DOWSING FOR WATER

Dowsing is simply water-divining, although some dowsers can also trace electrical cables, minerals, and oil. To the extent that it is no longer regarded as especially paranormal, dowsing has become accepted in the modern world. Traditionally, a forked stick is held out by a dowser as he or she walks through the countryside. If water is nearby, usually under the earth, the dowsing rod twitches. It has been suggested that dowsers are particularly sensitive to the Earth's magnetic field. However, some dowsers have found water by holding a pendulum over a map.

THE TAROT

The Tarot is a special deck of cards used for divination. Instead of the four suits of hearts, spades, diamonds and clubs of a deck of playing cards, the Tarot deck uses suits of cups, swords, wands and discs. Each suit has an additional court card. The Tarot deck also contains 22 greater trumps known as the Major Arcana. All the cards have symbolic associations as well as their apparent meaning. The different Tarot decks offer different interpretations. The Magician, for example, could mean willpower or skill. During a Tarot reading the cards are laid face down in certain positions to focus on different aspects of the subject's life. They are then turned over and interpreted.

THE I CHING

One of the oldest oracle books in the world, the Chinese *I Ching* or *Book of Changes* has lasted in its present form for at least 3000 years. Divination based on the *I Ching* does not predict specific events. Instead, it shows possible outcomes of certain actions. It is composed of 64 hexagrams in different combinations of six broken or unbroken lines. Using random activities such as drawing straws from a bundle or flipping a coin, a hexagram is produced and interpreted using the *I Ching*.

 FOOD FOR THOUGHT

Some divination methods, such as cartomancy or tea-leaf reading, involve interpretation of random effects. Others study a quality of the person seeking information (the 'querent'), as in palmistry or astrology. The difference between them is an important one. It is easier to believe that the querent's character might express itself through the lines on their palm, or might be influenced by the time of year of their birth, than that their presence can affect the fall of cards or twigs. It is also possible that the random methods of divination are used to give the diviner time to assess a person's character and to formulate an appropriate prediction.

DREAMS & VISIONS

Scientists are still investigating the processes of the unconscious mind. In his analysis of how the unconscious works, the forerunner of modern psychology, Sigmund Freud (1856-1939) paid special attention to the role of dreams. A Swiss psychologist, Carl Jung (1875-1961), later proposed that everyone shared a collective unconscious in which certain archetypal images recur, each with its own symbolism. Until the twentieth century, there was no concerted study of the human psyche. Psychology (study of the mind), like neuroscience (study of the brain), is still a young science. Parapsychology (study of psychic phenomena) draws on these other sciences but there is still much to be discovered.

KUBLA KHAN'S PLEASURE DOME

In 1797, the poet Samuel Taylor Coleridge composed 300 lines of poetry while in an opium-induced sleep. When he woke he could remember the poem and began to write it down but after being interrupted by a visitor he was unable to recall the rest of the poem. There are many instances of other writers, musicians, and artists gaining inspiration from their dreams. Parapsychologists have speculated that the sense of PSI (paranormal sensory information) is not as strong as the senses of touch, taste, smell, hearing, and sight. Being weaker, it functions better when there are no distractions, such as while a person sleeps.

SLEEP RESEARCH

Studies conducted on sleeping people indicated they were more susceptible to receiving psychic messages while in their REM period of sleep. Experiments involved a psychic transmitting images to a sleeping psychic at different stages of a sleep cycle. Woken after each stage, the person could recall the images more successfully after REM sleep.

REM SLEEP

The mind is active and people dream during the rapid eye movement (REM) stages of deep sleep. The body goes through five stages from deep to light sleep. During deep sleep, the body repairs itself. People dream every time they sleep although they might not remember their dreams. A technique known as lucid dreaming trains the sleeping mind to control the progress of dreams.

ANALYSIS OF DREAMS

There have been many theories about dreams. Ancient peoples believed they were messages from the gods. Freud, one of the first scientists who tried to explain dreaming, thought dreams were the wishes of the unconscious mind. More recently, Jung (right) wrote that in dreams people harness their creativity and come to terms with their fears. Modern sleep research tends to indicate that dreams are the result of the firing of neurons in the brain to help in the process of storing memories. Dreams are closely linked with the study of psychic phenomena because both are workings of the mind which is only partly understood.

OUT-OF-BODY EXPERIENCES

Many people have reported having near-death or out-of-body experiences, and commonly describe this as seeing a bright light pulling the soul away from the body. When the person is revived they often report having watched their own unconscious body being brought back to life. This 'astral' body is claimed to be identical to the physical body but is transparent and shining. Ancient writings describe this phenomenon as a supernatural power that can be gained through magic or meditation. Sceptics prefer to ascribe it to hallucination or delusion.

 FOOD FOR THOUGHT

All of these dream and vision phenomena can be attributed to the mind behaving oddly when it is on the edge of consciousness or beyond. Surrealist artists such as Salvador Dali deliberately induced this state in themselves. They believed it put them in touch with a higher level of reality and produced images intended to speak directly to their unconscious, perhaps drawing on universal symbols of a collective unconscious. Most people probably think they dream complex, strange, and interesting stories that would make wonderful films or books. Dreams are never easy to write down when you've woken up, though!

EXPERIMENTS OF THE MIND

Parapsychology is the study of extraordinary mental phenomena, such as telepathy, that are experienced by human beings yet seem to have no physical cause. Many scientists are suspicious of parapsychology because it has become associated, wrongly, with other paranormal events such as alien abductions. Parapsychology research includes investigating extrasensory perception (ESP) which is the ability to receive information not available to the accepted five senses; psychokinesis (PK) which is the ability to alter the state of physical objects by mental activity alone; and out-of-body experiences. The study of parapsychology assumes that the potential of the human mind has been underestimated.

TELEPATHY

Paranormal research has recorded many instances of telepathy occurring in everyday life. Close family relationships, especially between twins, tend to increase the likelihood of telepathic connection. Some experiments in which the participants try to communicate over long distances have achieved impressive results. However, if ESP is some kind of mental radio, it is proving very difficult to tune. Despite the high success rates, experiments have yet to prove the existence of viable telepathic communication.

PHOTOGRAPHING AURAS

Many mediums have claimed they can see an aura of light around the human body. In 1939, a Russian engineer, Semyon Kirlian developed a diagnostic technique that could sense heat and electro-magnetic fields. He photographed these auras using an electric coil, an aluminium plate and photosensitive film covered by glass. His pictures showed people surrounded by a coloured nimbus of light.

MILITARY APPLICATIONS OF PSI

Ever since the days when magic was used to protect the tribe, psychic phenomena have been investigated as a potential military aid. During the Cold War (following World War II), the American and Russian governments conducted serious studies of paranormal sensory information (PSI) and how it could be used. For some years, a secret American Defense project at the Pentagon, known as operation Stargate, has been rumoured to be training psychics to use their abilities to see into enemy bases and to attempt to cause mental confusion in foreign military leaders.

JOSEPH RHINE

In 1927, Dr Joseph Rhine and his wife, Louisa, started the first investigation into ESP at Duke University in North Carolina. This was the beginning of the science of parapsychology. Rhine invented the term ESP and spent 50 years researching the phenomenon. His work was first published in 1934. Scientists immediately found fault with his laboratory techniques and statistical analysis. Rhine successfully defended his techniques, but many thought his studies must have been experimental fraud.

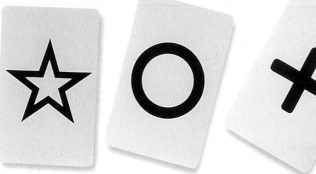

ZENER CARDS

ne of the earliest experiments in detecting psychic ability were Zener cards, a deck of 25 cards divided into five sets of five cards,
h with one of five different symbols on it. The cards were shuffled and, one at a time, a 'sender' would try to telepathically project
e symbol on each card to someone across the room. That person would attempt to 'see' what card the sender was projecting.
Rhine achieved a high success rate with this experiment under laboratory conditions. Some subjects were able to
name the entire deck of cards correctly and others could predict
in advance what order cards would
be shuffled into.

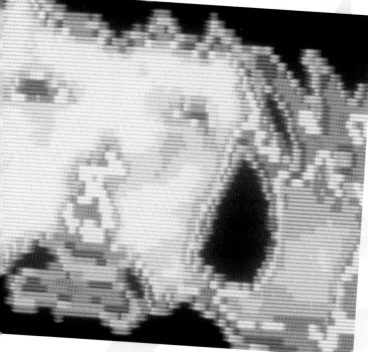

FOOD FOR THOUGHT

There is a one in five chance of correctly guessing which Zener symbol is being 'sent'. If an experiment was done using 100 cards the person 'receiving' is likely to guess right 20 times. Anything significantly above that may indicate the existence of ESP. Parapsychology research has rarely been taken seriously by mainstream science because of doubts about the validity of the experiments. It is difficult to design an experiment that makes it impossible for anyone to accuse the researcher of faking results. Indeed, some high-profile experiments have been faked, or interpreted with a particular bias. There is always a possibility that if a researcher is convinced that the phenomenon is genuine, they'll read what they want to believe into the results.

MESMERIZING MINDS

Franz Mesmer (1734-1815) was an Austrian physician. He believed the human body has magnetic properties that could be used to cure illness. Mesmer undertook public healings which involved connecting people by cords to a tub of water filled with iron filings. He achieved some notable successes but the scientific community remained unconvinced and he was denounced as an impostor. Although Mesmer's work was largely discredited, it paved the way for the study of hypnotism and the unconscious mind.

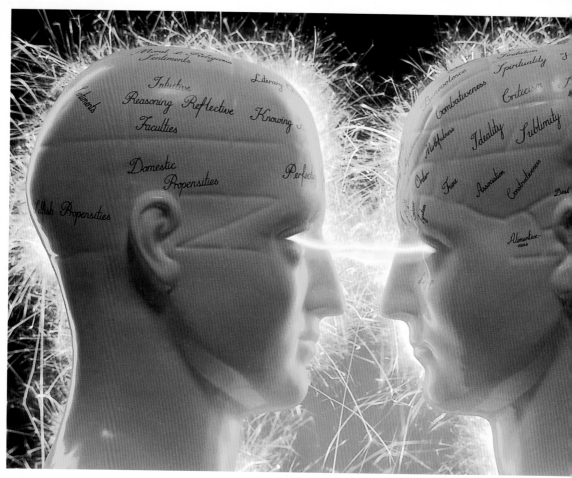

MENTAL RADIO

Recent paranormal research has been attempting to understand what happens when successful telepathic communication takes place. It may be possible to observe brain activity during a psychic episode by recording the pattern of brain-waves of an experimental subject. Some studies indicate there may be changes in alpha waves, the essential carrier signal for the operation of the mind, when psychic abilities are being used.

BIOGENETIC FORCE

In 1926, Russia was one of the first countries to do scientific research into psychic phenomena. Soviet scientists investigated the physical conditions necessary to enable the mind to transmit energy. In the 1970s, they did extensive studies of a Russian housewife called Nina Kulagina. Under controlled laboratory conditions, she was able to move objects, create burn marks, and increase the magnetic properties of objects without any physical contact with them. The force Kulagina apparently possessed has been called bioenergetics.

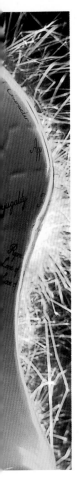

ESP & PK

The two most widely researched areas of psychic phenomena are extrasensory perception (ESP) and psychokinesis (PK). ESP is generally held to include telepathy (direct mind to mind communication), precognition (having knowledge of unplanned future events), and clairvoyance (having second sight, or the ability to foretell future events). PK is the movement of objects by the power of thought alone. PK may explain the apparent existence of poltergeists, ghosts who cause apparently untouched objects to break or levitate. It has been suggested that a teenager in a highly charged mental response to emotional problems could cause spontaneous PK.

GANZFELD EXPERIMENTS

The ganzfeld (total field) experiment was designed by parapsychologists to counter claims of experimental error.

To achieve a relaxed and receptive state, subjects were put into an environment free of all sensory influences from sight, sound, and touch.

A sender then attempted to telepathically communicate a randomly-selected image to the receptive person.

The receiver reported aloud all their thoughts, images, feelings, and impulses. The ganzfeld experiment achieved a high success rate. More subjects successfully projected and received images than would be predicted by the theory of probability.

RANDOM NUMBERS – DEFINITE RESULTS

Since electronic and computer technology became widespread, parapsychologists have conducted a series of experiments on the relationships between mind, matter, and energy. One such experiment measured the human ability to influence a random element, such as which number will be cast when a die is thrown. Random number generator (RNG) machines produce an electrical datastream that a test subject cannot modify by any physical means. Experiments established statistically that most humans *can* influence which numbers will come up randomly. The success rate seems higher at full moon; a time when magnetism in the brain may be affected by the Earth's magnetic field.

PSYCHOKINESIS

In the 1920s, Baron Albert von Schrenk-Notzing, an investigator of the paranormal, worked with Stanislava Tomczyk (right) and Willy Schneider to convince scientific observers and members of the English Society for Psychical Research that it was possible to levitate objects by no known physical means. Neither psychics nor Schrenk-Notzing were ever suspected of fraud.

PLACES OF POWER

Despite all the research into the subject, psychic phenomena remain an enigma. We cannot say with any certainty whether or not they genuinely exist or how they function but, just as our ancestors were, we are fascinated by psychic power and its potential uses. Over the centuries, the mystery of psychic phenomena has inspired many attempts to harness powers of the unknown. The legacy of those attempts is scattered across the world in the form of places of power. Some are natural sites in the landscape that are considered sacred. Others were built as a centre for religious beliefs, magical practices, or primitive superstitions. These ancient places are thought to symbolize psychic forces which we do not yet understand.

LINES OF POWER

Ley lines are channels of power that supposedly run all over the Earth. Some people believe dowsers can harness these forces to help them find water or metals. It has been suggested that ley lines may have been constructed by primitive man or an ancient advanced civilization, or are simply natural features of the Earth. Large monuments or standing stones often indicate the presence of ley lines nearby. It has also been suggested that ley lines may be detectable by variations in radio waves. In England, ley lines are believed to cross Glastonbury Tor (above), a place of great religious significance.

MAGIC OF THE ANCIENTS

The pyramids at Giza are some of the oldest surviving man-made structures in the world. They were built before 2500 BC by Egyptian pharaohs to entomb their mummified bodies and the valuable possessions that accompanied them into the afterlife to signify how rich and powerful they were. From the dimensions of the Great Pyramid modern mathematicians have worked out that ancient Egyptians knew the value of pi, the number of days Earth takes to circle the sun, and the dates of important events in the future. Recently, it has been suggested that the position of the pyramids in relation to one another is identical to the layout of stars in the constellation of Orion.

SACRED SITES OF THE ANCESTORS

Uluru (formerly Ayers Rock) in the Northern Territory of Australia is the largest single rock formation in the world and is a place of strong spiritual significance to the Aboriginal people. Many of the stories concerning Uluru are secret and are never repeated to outsiders. Around Uluru are many ancestral sites and out of respect for Aboriginal beliefs, the Australian government has restricted tourist access to them.

STANDING STONES

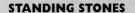

Stonehenge in Britain was built around 1200 BC but we do not know for what purpose. It may have been an astronomical observatory, a Druid religious centre, or a burial ground. In 1977, the Dragon Project was established to study electrical and magnetic forces around Stonehenge and similar monuments. There are many other standing stone monuments in the world. Some of the most impressive are Carnac in Brittany, Msoura in Morocco, and at Lake Turkana in Kenya.

FOOD FOR THOUGHT

Everyone feels a sense of awe and mystery when at one of these tremendous places of power. You don't have to share the beliefs of the people who built them, or those who use them today, to be amazed by the vision, dedication, effort, and genius that went into their construction. One of the most valuable things to remember about the power of the mind is that our ancestors, even if they had different beliefs to us, were just as intelligent and capable of achieving great things as we are.

DID YOU KNOW?

In Poland, a painting of the Madonna was once slashed with swords by a group of Hussites in 1430. Despite repeated attempts to repair the painting the slashes have always reappeared.

During a laboratory experiment in psychokinesis (PK) a piece of blank paper was left in a typewriter which was then guarded against all possibilities of anyone using it. Some time later, the paper was examined and the following unsigned verse was found.

A clever man, W.E. Cox
Made a really remarkable box
In it, we, with PK
In the usual way
Wrote, spite of bands, seals
and locks.

THE MAGICIAN.

New Zealand's rugby team, the All Blacks, perform a ceremonial ritual called the haka taparahi, prior to all their matches. In the tradition of the Maori people, the energetic chant and dance is intended to bring the team good fortune in the match.

Ouija is a combination of the French and German words for Yes.

In the Old Testament of the Bible, the prophet Elisha is said to have sent his spirit into the tent of a Syrian king to frustrate his plans to destroy the Israelites.

The most astounding story about a famous twentieth century Italian priest called Padre Pio was his bilocation, the ability to be in two places at the same time. One night, Padre Pio apparently knocked on the door of the Archbishop of Montevideo in Uruguay to inform him that one of his priests was dying. Sometime later, the Archbishop met Pio who confirmed that he had been in Uruguay that night, although he had never physically left Italy.

The Australian Skeptics group is offering $A80,000 to anyone who can prove the existence of ESP, telepathy, or telekinesis. The prize has been on offer since 1980 and is still waiting to be won.

You can find out more about the supernatural on the Internet. Why not check out these websites?
www.skeptics.com.au/features/chalenge.htm
www.skepdic.com
www.parascope.com

ACKNOWLEDGEMENTS
We would like to thank: Helen Wire and Elizabeth Wiggans for their assistance.
Copyright © 1999 ticktock Publishing Ltd.
First published in Great Britain by ticktock Publishing Ltd., The Offices in the Square, Hadlow, Tonbridge, Kent TN11 0DD, Great Britain.
All rights reserved.
No part of this publication may be reproduced, stored in a retrieval system, or transmitted in any form or by any means electronic, mechanical, photocopying, recording or otherwise, without prior written permission of the copyright owner.
A CIP catalogue record for this book is available from the British Library. ISBN 1 86007 105 8 (paperback). ISBN 1 86007 141 4 (hardback).

Picture research by Image Select. Printed in Hong Kong.

Picture Credits: t = top, b = bottom, c = centre, l = left, r= right, OFC = outside front cover, OBC = outside back cover, IFC = inside front cover

AKG; 3br, 2tl, 6/7b, 10cb, 12tl, 16c, 21c, 24tl, 31cr. Ann Ronan @ Image Select; 2bl, 4/5t, 8tl, 15c, 17tr. British Museum; 13t. Colorific; 12/13c. Corbis; 4/5b, 8bl, 12/13b & OBC, 18bl, 26cl, 26tl, 26/27c. e.t.archive; 6/7t. Fortean; 2c, 5tr, 6c, 6/7c, 8/9b, 10l, 10/11ct, 11bl, 14 (main pic), 14/15t, 15b, 15tr, 16b, 22bl, 22/23b, 26b, 27b, 26/27t, 28cb, 28/29c, 29br, 29rt, 30tl. Gamma; IFC, 7t. Geoscience; 4bl. Image Select; 9tr, 16/17b, 18c, 25tr, 31t. Images; 18tl. Science Photo Library; 24bl, 24/25c. Telegraph Colour Library; OFC (main pic), 8c. Tony Stone; 12bl, 19tr, 18/19c, 20, 22c, 22tl, 25c, 30/31 (main).Werner Foreman; 3tr.

Every effort has been made to trace the copyright holders and we apologize in advance for any unintentional omissions.
We would be pleased to insert the appropriate acknowledgement in any subsequent edition of this publication.

snapping-turtle
guide